THE WHERE AND WHEN

THE WHERE AND WHEN

MALCOLM CARSON

All rights reserved. No part of this work covered by the copyright herein may be reproduced or used in any means—graphic, electronic, or mechanical, including copying, recording, taping, or information storage and retrieval systems—without written permission of the publisher.

Printed by imprintdigital
Upton Pyne, Exeter
www.digital.imprint.co.uk

Typesetting and cover design by narrator
www.narrator.me.uk
info@narrator.me.uk
033 022 300 39

Published by Shoestring Press
19 Devonshire Avenue, Beeston, Nottingham, NG9 1BS
(0115) 925 1827
www.shoestringpress.co.uk

First published 2019
© Copyright: Malcolm Carson
© Cover photographs: Malcolm Carson

The moral right of the author has been asserted.

ISBN 978-1-912524-31-0

ACKNOWLEDGEMENTS

Acknowledgements are due to the editors of the following where some of these poems, or versions of them, first appeared:

The Interpreter's House
Obsessed with Pipework
Cumbria Wildlife Trust
The High Window
Orbis
Poetry Salzburg Review
London Grip

In memory of my brother
Timothy Joseph Carson

CONTENTS

Where the Gelt gathers	1
A rural symposium	2
A kitchen visit	3
For the best	4
Ghost bikes	5
Not that Godric	6
Good husbandry	7
Great Crested Newts	9
Lincolnshire Orchids	10
On Wittenham Clumps	11
Ramsden and the coal man	12
Robin	14
The Owl and George MacBeth	15
Edgar regards the politicians	16
North	17
South	18
East	19
West	20
The dream revisited	21
The Old Byre Gallery	22
The croft	24
Looking nice	25
A sense of duty	26
Autographs	27
Deuce	28
Ellmann's *Joyce*	29
The importance of elbows	30
The lead	31
The Silent Sibling	32
The Toby Jugs	33
Edgar at harvest time	34
Edgar and the geese	35
The boat	36
The Guide	37
easyPrague	38
Edgar and his chronicler	40

The man who married a rock	41
Butterflies	42
Hindu funeral	43
Verandah	44
Pack horse	45
Mona Lisa, Mona Lisa	46
Glacier	47
Edgar revisits the shore	48

WHERE THE GELT GATHERS

Where the Gelt gathers here on broken fell,
forgotten except by those who maunder

along tracks of mines and hillsides pocked
with waste heaps, I come among

wild cattle whose gaze you'd best avoid,
the startled snipe and startling grouse.

No chance of dramatic view, tasteful panorama:
just the fellsides shifting colour as you watch,

catch breath, run on. You might though
be amazed by kingfishers' embroidered seam

along the wooded gill, or harrier's doomed flight.
Yet all the time the Gelt is swelling, drawing

mists, storms, dew, and even sweat through turf and bog,
sieving age and aspiration as it sees fit.

A RURAL SYMPOSIUM

'Aye,' he said, shifting
his weight
on to the other elbow,
heavy as a sack
of spuds.

Silence.

'Aye,' came in answer
from the other,
looking beyond
the optics
and his mirrored self.

Silence.

A sup of beer.
A check of fob-watch
against bar clock.

'Aye,' said either,
confident in their confederacy,
unspoken understanding
of the seasons,
vicissitudes of harvests,
how cattle fare,
the loneliness of turning land.

'Aye.'

A KITCHEN VISIT

When the treecreeper came
fretting in my kitchen,
he—perhaps she—
studied window frames,
tops of cupboards where
dust and iron pans
cohabit in happy neglect,
shat a bit on sills,
maybe perplexed by lack
of barky substance whereby
to grip, point up and needle
out impossible insects.
And when she—perhaps he—
found the rim of the fish tank,
it was quiescent enough
to be cradled out to flight,
bamboozled by the golden creatures
blubbing beneath that circled
in equal bewilderment.
Such collisions of nature
in our equable domesticity.

FOR THE BEST

It was something they'd agreed upon: for the best,
they said, since neither seemed to welcome proximity
anymore, 'contiguity' he remembered
from his DEFRA days, and farms in quarantine.

Moving to the next bedroom was easy enough:
an unencumbered sprawling at night, no worrying
about snoring, quilt sharing, or odoriferous interruptions.
So nights passed in bliss, despite the odd

reaching out for comfort, a snuffling of regret.
Until the day when, overslept, he found
his breakfast there, a commode, and a fond note
to tell him, such was the success of the sleeping experiment,

separate quarters were now in place. He was sure to agree,
it said, that all's for the best. The bedroom is capacious,
affording splendid views to the garden, laid
to lawn, in agent's speak, and discreet, discrete

apartments were the order of the day. Such
was his compliance, his desire to accommodate,
he gave it a go, and found he quite liked it,
ignoring that, like the bean plants on schoolroom sill,

he grew pale and limp, 'etiolated', he recalled, just as
the stem doubled over, starved of love and sustenance.

GHOST BIKES

All movement stopped that day
as they rolled toward the sun.

A sudden separation.
The riders torn away

as if they were an impudence.
Saddles cooled.

Wheels lost their torsion,
gurning, the frame distressed,

bereft of purpose. Gear shifters
divorced the guiding bars,

and chainset uncoupled.

                        Patched up,
they stand at Moota ghosting

a journey only partly made,
lives only partly lived.

NOT THAT GODRIC

Næs þæt na se Godric   þe ða guðe forbeah

The Battle of Maldon

...forbeah—so Godric fled,
wretched in itself to desert
his lord, his companion

of the hearth, the meadhall,
when the enemy came,
broke the shield wall

to let in marauders
demanding gelt, servitude.
And on the steed

of Byrhtnoð, just slain,
leading many to think
the worst, their own lord

leaving the field: Godric,
cowardly son of Odda
fleeing from the fight.

But it was not that Godric
who hewed and menaced
until felled by Viking blow,

no flight for him
to his fastness,
Æþelgares son, no shame

in his name who followed
his lord, courage stropped
in slaughter, no, not that Godric.

GOOD HUSBANDRY

Setting the bulbs,
'They'll need a hard frost,'
he muttered,

checking the right way up
before knuckling down
the soft earth bedding.

'Funny that, how cold
prompts the growth.
Some chemical reaction,

I suppose.' He stood,
unstiffened his back
against his fork,

stretched and looked
toward the cottage door.
How closed to him it seemed.

'It's a shame a rime
doesn't work for us,
start us up to loving more.'

As the curtain blinked,
he knew she'd been
watching, waiting,

tending her quibbles,
resentment, disappointment
in their loneliness.

Too much cold, he thought,
more like a permafrost.
No bloom's going to break

through that crust.
I'll cut her a cabbage.
She'll like that.

GREAT CRESTED NEWTS

He lifted up the log carefully
as you might a fledgling
—I have a licence he tells us.
We peer down, hushed,
and see the young
like apostrophes in time.
The cameras snap. We talk
as though above a cot,
amazed at good fortune.
He holds them out for us,
gives his warmth, then
slips them beneath the log,
back into prehistory.

LINCOLNSHIRE ORCHIDS

'Orchids!' he posted proudly
at the purple Tufted Vetch,
common as muck in my garden.

'Orchids!' he posted proudly
at the Himalayan Balsam,
promiscuous on waterways.

How to disabuse him, or
should I even try? What's gained
if vetch and stinking balsam

give him delight, pride
in his park? So let them
be orchids, Lincolnshire

Orchids, now found by roadsides
everywhere where flowers defy
being labelled, give happiness.

ON WITTENHAM CLUMPS

For Carole and John Blythe

Above the skylark in a haze
of song, kites circle for cadavers.
The wolfhound would be
off its leash and at
the throat of soft retriever.

Beneath the slick of grass
a history to pick at:
cattle jaws, quernstones,
spindlewhorls and loomweights,
swan's neck pin, struck flints,
sifted from time's midden.

Trek around the hills,
build desultory shelters,
squat on fallen beech,
watch the silky Thames
past darkening abbey,
and others flying dreams.

You can only fancy the savage fort,
the continuous watch against
loss of ground just gained.

RAMSDEN AND THE COAL MAN

With his blazer and silver buttons,
double breasted, his wonderful
trainset, bought at cost
by his dad through his own shop,
he was always different.
Yet we were mates for a while,
biking back from school,
his much better, of course.
There was envy, not unreasonably,
a decent footballer too.

But then that day.
The coal lorry passing us
in the narrow lane,
grammar school boys
in blazers and caps,
them with blackened faces.
'You need to get a wash!'
my friend's leery remark.
A shuddering halt,
an angry coal man
out of his cab, cap raised,
ready to swipe coal dust
over Ramsden's retreating smile.
'That's good honest dirt
from honest work!'
A stammered apology,
and a parting of the ways,
lorry door slammed,
bikes remounted.

I hear it still, that voice, assertive,
proud, against the shopkeeper's son.

**

I've seen him since in his local news,
his supermarket smile,
combination shirt and tie,
passing down his empire to his sons,
and wonder if that day ever dusted
coal on his awareness too.

ROBIN

How the robin sings
when day is stripped of light
and trees of leaves,
when boughs lace a sky
turned to ice.
Its clarity thrills
across an empty road,
while thrush and blackbird
hunker down, depressed.
Sing again, my beauty!
God knows we need you.
Sing again!

THE OWL AND GEORGE MACBETH

Poems about owls had hunted my sleep
that night, but one made me blink awake
to remember his name. I stalked it
in the waking hours, ran through
an undergrowth, but off it skulked.
I pictured him read: round glasses
like the wise owl's, soft 'r',
three-piece suit and the music of
'hoovering over the floor of the wood'.
I remembered the poems from Oby,
his too-soon death, but
I slipped back with failure.

It was then outside my window
the tawny owl came,
ke-wick, bringing with it
the fat mouse of his name.

EDGAR REGARDS THE POLITICIANS

I have seen them peeking out of holes, watching
if the land is clear before they utter
reckless things, draw back, and let the caterwauling
crowd take up their cry. Only then
from burrows do they emerge, seeming to
reflect the popular will with mock reluctance,
forced to heed 'the common good'. They leer
and fawn and seem offended by obstructions
from dissenters, impeders of the people's will.
Behind the scenes, they skulk in improbable liaisons
which will unravel upon the hour when chance's
easy option allows for seeing off
a rival's threat. (Those sisters know a thing
or two, as does my brother whom they crave.
Such concupiscence!) Yet still I hope that in
their moil they either tire or get found out
and perish by each other's hand. Or yet
will nature have vengeance? Too much to hope? Perhaps,
but what else if there's to be a rebalancing
of order after the dark hours of a disordered world?

NORTH

Northumberland, to the north of Humber and all I knew.
We travelled in the dark one year, Armstrong Siddeley
packed with cases, sandwiches for that unwonted
route to Ireland. And then dawn breaking on landscapes
I'd never known, imagined: rugged, in yellows,
russets, streaked with silver, the sky screaming
its unfamiliarity.

It's where I live now, the North, those mountains
and moors are known. Yet that journey still emerges
just like the fell tops appearing glorious
in the sun above the mat of fogs as we cross
from visits to the south of Humber, growing strange.

SOUTH

We'd lean in the tiled queue for the best
fish and chips in that haddock town, listen in on banter,
admire the batter, scan the posters for
Vern's Away Days to the Lochs and Highlands,
or *Cliff in Sheffield*. 'Been on your holidays?'
'Yeah, down south' the coiffured reply
of erstwhile Miss Evening Telegraph,
now proprietress of that stainless emporium.
'Whereabouts down south?'
A moment's hesitation, then: 'All the way.'

Haddock, chips, mushy peas, fish cakes with parsley,
skate wings (to be requested on entry)
deferred then to visions of that wondrous pair
in pristine whites, caravanning over channels,
borders, ignoring isthmus and the scourge
of tempests, down Andes, Patagonia, over
glacial boulders, frazil ice, the katabatic winds,
feasting only on pemmican, and powder snow,
laughing at sastrugi and snotsicles,
to arrive at the magnetic pole, ambition sated, heave a sigh:
'That's the South done, then,' turn round
and back to frying the North Sea's best.
'Open or wrapped?'

With acknowledgments to Marklew's fish shop, Grimsby, and Sir Ranulph Fiennes.

EAST

East is where my life came up
slowly, uncertainly, in a seaside town.
East is where the planes took off,
lumbering over the flat coast,
often not returning
to our county of marsh and aerodromes.

East was always where we came from,
where no one else had ever been,
and where we'd always have to
explain where it was. And being that,
we took delight in leading them
where our fancy might take us in turn.

WEST

'Out West' is what we say
of Cumbria parts some treat
as if they mattered less.
It's where the slag heaps meet
the sea, and cliffs crumble,
black against mesmeric
tides. Or else where towns'
grandeur has peeled away.
Industry's largely nuclear now,
dependency that enthrals.
The villages where mines grew,
fall back, scrat for meaning,
wrong side of Lakeland beauty.
Easy though to assume
that West is only where
the sun will set, or where
ambition fades. There's something
to be said for being out
of sight, and simply getting on.

THE DREAM REVISITED

Skye, May 2016

It wouldn't be like this most days,
sun on the loch, the distant point,
clear as a blade, where clans had met
for mutual slaughter—such romance—
byres now as galleries.
He knew the roads' rise and fall,
the passing places where bog cotton
drifts along the fence. He'd loved it:
visits to crofts, tracking the news
along his skein of friends.
Imagine though, he said,
reluctant in his wisdom,
a fracture in that weave,
how alone you'd be,
through careless word or deed,
misplaced humour. And then
the winter.
It wasn't what he wanted,
common sense, on days
like this, when thyme scents
the breeze and all seems perfect.

THE OLD BYRE GALLERY

They've gone
the snorting beasts

steam off
buttressed flanks,

sweating hay,
furtive rat, or

brazen. This a bank
against winter's

worst, loch's bite.
All were hoarded

here, family's gelt.
Now walls are painted

pristine white
the better to offset

frames wherein
the foam of threshing

sea is shuttered
on a moment.

Menus offer 'slow
roasting meats',

scones and soups
freshly dressed with

local herbs. Skylights
defy the year's

weather, letting in
the light on how

they hope it will
all go well, anxious

lives invested in
a byre, and trade

that passes by
the slated drive,

or crunches up to
augment their gelt.

THE CROFT

for Jock and Morag Ross

'This,' he says, 'is a croft,'
as though to correct my misconception
as of a charming cottage, slightly ruined,
a backdrop of clearances. His arm

sweeps from the bungalow where children's slide
lies toppled beneath the washing line,
down across the strip of meadow
to the shore. The spread of buttercups

glows along our path, the child
on his shoulders, the collie with the buoy
on a rope, herding it to where the scooter
lies forgotten, the oystercatcher

cries alarm. 'Yes, the croft goes
into the water, to low tide line,'
he tells us, though we don't know
what to make of that. We gaze

out across the bay, watch dulse
surge and suck as oystercatcher settles
for photographs. Turning back he says
the pasture will be cut before long,

and what the price might be, stops
with child, clutched by her wellies, to pull
pernicious ragwort. 'There's a fine for leaving it.
See the orchids! We look out for those.'

LOOKING NICE

It would be nice, we all agreed, to have
my mother's grave spick and span ready
for the burial of the newly dead hard by
the long buried. We'd taken cloths, water
in a bottle, Stardrops, working beside
gravediggers, who measured the depth
of where they'd put him, in an hour or two.
We scrubbed and scraped to get off bird shit
enamelled on to marble, used a 50p piece.
'We're not there yet,' our neighbours called,
checking the depth with measuring stick.
Swilling down the stones, we placed some flowers,
keen it looked its best to welcome the dead
next door. We said farewell to our companions,
avoided slipping into 'See you later.'

A SENSE OF DUTY

He had overseen the digging of the grave
only hours before. Now he stood, head bowed,

wanting anonymity, while the vicar
did his bit. Distress was real among

those who loved, dropped single flowers
while he, hands crossed in front, pinioned that moment.

The webbing straps, the putlogs that took the coffin's weight
were the tools of his trade, as was his composure.

And when all was done, he stood apart, waiting, quiet,
ready to do his duty, as the rags of the party
fluttered off between the yews and waiting cars.

AUTOGRAPHS

Not so much the signatures,
but more the where and when.

Dickie Valentine's at Cleethorpes Ritz
for my sister, John Spink's dad

—'By hook or by crook…' aiming
to be 'the last in this book'.

My mother's 'My love is like a cabbage…',
my dad's signed off like a prescription.

The footballers: Dynamo Prague's Art Deco
when the curtain was Iron, when

Blundell Park was the best of all grounds.
The Busby Babes' scattered

through my book as they have been
through my life. When players'

writing was as cultured as Johnny Haynes,
when personal letters came

with 'Sorry it's taken so long.' Then some
we didn't want—teachers',

those teams' below us, girl friends'
because we knew they,

and we, would move on. They're stacked on
my desk now, occasionally opened,

and will stay like that until another
where and when is scribbled.

DEUCE

She would never have imagined she'd fall for him,
not in a million years, and when she did

her friends were agog. 'How can you? He's so dull!
Worthy, yes, but dull. And solid.'

'I know,' she said, 'but I love him. And dullness
isn't a bad thing in a good man, and

he is a good man.' So, dazzled by
his dullness, she took him as her love, leaving

a gawping society, tennis racquets dangling,
bewildered, while she exulted,
he dully, duly, was delighted.

ELLMANN'S *JOYCE*

I must tell my mother
how much I love it
now I have got round to
that daunting blue tome
I've always meant to read,
its spine creased from her
afternoons in the sun
in her chaotic garden,
windows, doors open,
indifferent to burglars,
as she lived the times
again. Must tell her.
Oh, but of course,
she's twenty years dead.

THE IMPORTANCE OF ELBOWS

In an age that seems the stuff of imagining,
her teacher warned my aunt: *Fiona McComb,
don't lean on your elbows! No one will want
to marry a young lady with ugly elbows.*

The ladies' academy knew its role, catering
for aspirants in their own class, corseting
any wayward inclination that might diminish
the chances of a suitable marriage.

Yet Belfast's eligible elite were quite prepared
for employing elbows as they saw fit
to dispatch covetous rivals
for the match of choice, making sure

that they for one would not be out at elbow.
Others though gazed beyond the confines
of sound etiquette where careers
beckoned, giving the elbow to dependence.

THE LEAD

Watching her walk her dog, hand it
the lead to bring them home,
I thought of how my father once used
our Tinker's lead to thrash my legs
for minor disobedience, and how
our beloved dog might have cowered,
its bond with us misused. Unfair
perhaps to hold my father still
for that.
        Should I put aside
that weal on memory, think only
of the walks, the beach, mind's happier
perambulations? No need for guilt
for we can't whistle back such thoughts,
however great the pain.

THE SILENT SIBLING

i.m. Rosemary Adeline Carson

They never talked about her, the one
who didn't see the light of day,
hidden from us for our own good,
perhaps, or else too painful to recall.
Only when our mother's days
were thinning did she reveal we'd had
an older sister, that my father had cried.

And when we found the grave
—a solitary stone, no name engraved—
it was across from where
our mother lay, silence
shared across a muddy path,
the graves greening among
the yews and composted flowers.

THE TOBY JUGS

She came for the toby jugs
when our mother died,

took them off the staircase
shelf where they'd grinned

and gurned at all that passed.
Why she'd want them

we couldn't fathom,
those grotesqueries.

One you could at least
wind up to play 'A health

unto you, gentlemen'
until its song was snapped.

What she did with them
we never knew for with

those simpering jugs, she took
herself, packed away

all contact as her inheritance.
Photos were sent, cards

and 'Best Wishes' until
'not known at this address'

defined how she felt,
though, worst of all, we never

knew why, could only surmise:
her bequest to us.

EDGAR AT HARVEST TIME

I assume a role by the gate,
leaning in my fustian, watching
with inconsequence the gleaners
among the stubble, the castled stooks,
or where the trailer leaked
its precious load. Meagre allowances
for backs near-broken from bearing
sacks up ladders that creaked
as much as bones. Small birds
move in behind their shuffle
—all is safely gathered in.
There will be celebrations,
a reckoning of good process,
loyalty, and so with them
I'll throw off morbidity,
ignore life's disproportion until
such time as I can deal justly.

EDGAR AND THE GEESE

How I love their call
that reaches into
my darkest hour.
I may be engrossed
in such important things,
yet must draw
apart and gaze into
the winter sky,
seek out their echelon
and soar toward them.
They might settle,
if I'm in luck,
on these sodden fields
where grass invites
replenishment,
or else pass over to
Solway's reaches
where bitter winds
and cruel skies seem
as nothing at journey's end.
I will take comfort
for my afflictions,
when the flight of geese
enriches so.

THE BOAT
Tivat, Montenegro

I love it here, joshing with these two,
a glass of wine or three, olives, nuts,
speaking loudly enough to impress
ourselves, others perhaps, I hope.

I look across to where she lies,
my beauty, a grand boat, sleek,
confident, statement of my success.
One among others, I grant you that,

where Saudis come and go,
but berthed to good effect.
And then she rings. Two minutes,
I reply, and stretching them to fifteen.

A tussle over the bill, each eager
to show he can, a mere bagatelle.
Back to the boat for me, drawbridge down,
onto my little castle, along the deck,

past galley, reception, dining,
sunpads and sundeck, designed
for my serenity. I have sonar
for detecting hazards, bridge systems

for where company might be found.
The lights come on at sunrise, a lovely sight
from the shore. The wine bar though looks good.
Now, where might she be?

THE GUIDE

Agrah, May 2017

How sceptical we were,
a tacky gewgaw where
the worst of tourist tat
would overwhelm
its cold beauty.

He asked us to hold back,
in the shade, let go
ahead the chattering,
and look.

We drew breath
and gazed. And gazed.

'Could you ever
get tired of this?'
I asked.

'This is my office. I never tire.'

He led us by the snapping crowd,
hot for selfies on the Taj backdrop.

He found us peace
in quiet corners.

'Take your time.'
We took on his calm:
it was enough to gaze.

easyPrague

i

Grave dug on grave
the dead bicker for space
in their allotment.
Names prinked in red and gold
on memorial walls encrypt
a tale we can only nod to.
Pick out a name then,
family, date of birth, extinction,
put it to the death place
you may have heard about.

ii

In the Spanish Synagogue
gold and red in the cupola
muffle the senses like dralon.
Seized goods were stored, souls
numbered, stripped and shelved
until collection time.
Families that had been stitched
into a glorious cloth were unpicked,
laid separate as squares,
rags for industrial parts.
We don the provided caps
in due reverence,
leave them by the door.

iii

In the National Gallery we are exhibits
observed by guardians moving round
soundless with a curiosity to protect
the hush of what they know is best
despite the change in weather in the street.
We lean to the titles, artist, weigh the date
of birth and death. Uniforms glide behind.

iv

Through the hollow market
the wind blows down
from quartered blocks
in serviceable suburbs.
In our tourist bed we hear
the bellows of easyStags
cacophony of easyHens
down Havelska to the gothic clock
in the elegant square.

EDGAR AND HIS CHRONICLER

Who are you who places me
in such odd circumstance,
in times incongruous to mine,
allows me to speak in language
I couldn't know? And then you dare
to fancy how I might feel
in time's disjuncture,
let alone when family turns upon itself.
Still, I'll not spin round on chance
of catching you spying behind
the transept column, or playing
wildfowler on Solway's flats,
for then would my adventures cease,
and I'd be folded back
into the pages of a play,
my story that of a grieving son,
a brother wronged, who,
though still victorious,
is just another in
a dramatis personae. Much better
to let you do as you will,
though the time may come
when I'll chide you
for too much liberty.
So, be careful how you tread,
whoever you are.

THE MAN WHO MARRIED A ROCK

I love its texture,
bulk, reassurance,
always there for me,
and I for it.

I clamber up its side;
it doesn't complain
or nag—yet
might upbraid me
—graininess helping
my ascent.

Standing on the top
we are one, both happy.

In monsoons, it changes
mood, dress,
glistens in silks,
colours chosen
for me.

I couldn't have
asked for better.

BUTTERFLIES

It was the butterflies above all,
warming on the stones.
The mountains' massif, the snows, peaks,
unthinkable crevasses enticed, repelled,
while purples, yellows, black and white
flitted near my feet, between rocks
where sweat glinted for a moment
and then was gone. Yet the butterflies
still dance, trip remembrance.

HINDU FUNERAL

Straw pyre
by water's edge.
A scree of relatives.
Flames carry belief
heavenward.

VERANDAH

The time of day
that verandahs
were invented for.

Washing drips
from the line,
some mountains shift
with the sun.

Just across, crows
aloft, consider the pines.

PACK HORSE

Slender ledge before light,
new snow. Head torches bob
and contour up ahead.
My strength goes—no surprise
after last night's gale
in my room, bad guts
from days before—a brief
paralysis, threatened
with a classic slide.

And then the pack horse.
Lifted on, I felt what
dependency means, giving in
a sort of luxury.
Wrapped in care, my legs
embrace the swaying belly,
hands buried beneath
the blanket saddle.

His heart now, surefootedness
on improbable rock.
Hours to reach the pass
where light gathered,
prayer flags embroidering
the moment's elation.

The horse stands relieved
of me, and me relieved.

MONA LISA, MONA LISA

How I love you,
your faded oleograph
here in the Himal
as inscrutable
as your smile
bestowing patronage
on trekkers,
guides, porters
regaling themselves.
Hotel owners too
adore you,
'Monah Lisha',
sanctify their hospitality
with what they think
we think is best
to guarantee
a traveller's preference
over 'Perfect View' or
'Beautiful Vista'.

GLACIER

It's hard to spot the glacier
except by reading backward.
The azure lake, its shoreline,
café, gift shop of sorts,
the necessary bridge
of salvaged logs
where the lake spills off.
Follow the feeder up
through scrags of boulders
beneath the brittle cliffs
to where you see
a softening of texture
as though of coffee grains,
a dirty smudge that's
all that's left of
Gangapurna's sighs.

EDGAR REVISITS THE SHORE

It was here, I remember,
I dug for bait. The tide

out beyond the creeks,
castles made by worms

giving away their safety
to probing forks.

I look across to pools
where the diggers were,

to breakwaters reaching
out to a rib of tide,

striations where curlew
probe, and waders

are set up by errant dog,
perfect in flighted alarm.

Where now 'Tom'?
On seeing this again,

do I need him still, or
will he persist despite

my best efforts to put behind
the time upon the heath?

Who's to know? As light
seeps with the tide,

my shadow lengthens
across the sand, stretching

with the minute until
it will extinguish in the gloom.

Yet I am glad I came,
for only by gazing at

the darkest hour, can Edgar
be himself. *Ripeness is all.*